DEMCO

Safe Kids
School Safety

Dana Meachen Rau

Marshall Cavendish
Benchmark
New York

Follow the rules in school.

School rules help keep you safe.

Class Rules

1. Treat each other with respect
2. Be in your seat when the bell rings with all materials ready.
3. Turn all assignments in on time.
4. Keep hands, feet and objects to yourself.
5. Eat food only in the cafeteria or patio area. Leave gum and candy at home.

Do not run in the halls.

You could crash into someone.

Keep your shoes tied.

Shoelaces can make you trip.

Carry scissors the right way.

Keep the points from hurting someone.

Never lean back in your chair.

You could fall and hit your head.

Stay with your class in a *fire drill*.

Then your teacher will know you are safe.

Be quiet when the teacher is talking.

Then you will hear her directions.

Wash your hands with soap and water.

Dirty hands spread *germs*.

Cover your nose and mouth when you sneeze.

You do not want to make someone else sick.

Do not share food at lunch.

Sit in your seat when you eat.

Watch out for the swings.

You could get kicked.

Never walk up the slide.

Someone else might be
coming down!

Be a safe kid at school.

Be Safe

fire drill

hall

lunch

scissors

shoelaces

slide **sneeze** **swings**

Challenge Words

fire drill A time to practice leaving the school in case of a real fire.

germs (jurmz) Tiny living things that can make you sick.

Index

Page numbers in **boldface** are illustrations.

About the Author

Dana Meachen Rau is the author of many other titles in the Bookworms series, as well as other nonfiction and early reader books. She lives in Burlington, Connecticut, with her husband and two children.

The author would like to thank Gwendolyn Hansen, RN, Lake Garda Elementary School, Burlington, Connecticut, for her help with this book.

With thanks to the Reading Consultants:

Nanci Vargus, Ed.D., is an Assistant Professor of Elementary Education at the University of Indianapolis.

Beth Walker Gambro is an Adjunct Professor at the University of Saint Francis in Joliet, Illinois.

Marshall Cavendish Benchmark
99 White Plains Road
Tarrytown, New York 10591-9001
www.marshallcavendish.us

Library of Congress Cataloging-in-Publication Data

Rau, Dana Meachen, 1971-
School safety / by Dana Meachen Rau.
p. cm. — (Bookworms: Safe kids)
Includes index.
Summary: "Identifies common hazards at school and advises how to deal with them"
—Provided by publisher.
ISBN 978-0-7614-4090-1
1. Schools—Safety measures—Juvenile literature. 2. Safety
education—Juvenile literature. I. Title.
LB2864.5.R38 2010
363.11'371—dc22
2008044935

Editor: Christina Gardeski
Publisher: Michelle Bisson
Designer: Virginia Pope
Art Director: Anahid Hamparian

Photo Research by Anne Burns Images

Cover Photo by *Photo Edit*/Michael Newman

The photographs in this book are used with permission and through the courtesy of:
SuperStock: pp. 1, 7, 28BR age fotostock; pp. 5, 28TC Mauritius; p. 11 Neal Slavin;
p. 15 Francisco Cruz. *Photo Edit*: p. 3 Mary Kate Denny; pp. 9, 28BL Christina Kennedy;
pp. 13, 28TL Tony Freeman; pp. 23, 29R David Young Wolf. *Corbis*: p. 17 Ralf-Finn Hestoft;
pp. 19, 29C Jose L. Pelaez; pp. 21, 28TR Owen Franken; p. 27 LWA-Dann Tardif.
Alamy: pp. 25, 29L Dave Porter.

Printed in Malaysia
1 3 5 6 4 2